BRIDGE TO A
BETTER LIFE

By
LAWRENCE HINCKLEY

DeVorss & Co., *Publishers*
P.O. Box 550, Marina Del Rey, CA 90291

ISBN: 0-87516-255-X

Printed in the United States of America
by Book Graphics, Inc., Marina del Rey, California

CONTENTS

TOWARD ENLIGHTMENT

PREFACE

Are you so successful in your business life that you have acquired an ulcer? When night comes do you settle down to a restful sleep induced by a tablet manufactured for this purpose? Are you so spiritually minded that you dress up and attend church on Easter Sunday? Do you feud with your neighbor?

Possibly your case of jitters and frustration is not as acute as the above; but unless you are enjoying every minute of every day, experiencing peace and love and happiness in your life, you are not claiming the divine heritage which God intends for you. You are not LIVING your religion.

I do not claim to be an expert on religion or religious philosophy and I am not a minister. My life has been that of an artist and businessman. But it seems to me that if religion is to count for something in our lives, it should be practical and helpful in solving everyday problems. I have studied the religions of the world, and especially the truths to be found in the New Testament. I have read numerous books by religious leaders of our time, and this little manuscript is the sum total of all this study boiled down to a few simple ideas. They have been a help to me and I would like to share them with you.

A sound basis for true happiness is a satisfactory spiritual concept. Do you believe in God? I am sure your reply to this question would be, "Of course I do." This being the case, just how deeply have you thought about this God in whom you believe? Try taking a paper and pencil and jotting down your concept of the Deity. You may be astonished at the confusion in your own mind.

You may conceive of God as Spirit, or as First Cause, or perhaps as some sort of super being who resides up in the sky. Some people think of Him as a stern king. To some fortunate mortals He dispenses health, prosperity and love; and to others He brings sickness, poverty and loneliness. Is your belief one of a God of love, and at the same time a God of wrath?

This last idea of the Almighty somewhat parallels the conception I had of Him for many years. Back in the days when I was a child in Sunday school, I remember picturing Him in my mind as a sort of super king with long white hair. His head was always adorned with a jeweled crown. He carried a scepter and was dressed in ethereal robes. I was told that He had His eye on me at all times, and I soon decided that this wasn't so much to protect me from harm as to keep an accurate check on my sins (of which I was assured I had many!) So many, in fact, that even at that early age, the chances of escaping the wrath to come seemed pretty slim indeed. My only hope then was to learn the Sunday school lesson, and see to it that I was present in class every week when the roll was called.

As I look back on these childhood experiences, I do not wonder that at maturity my idea of God was a pretty mixed up affair. The tragic thing about the situation is that hundreds of thousands of men and women carry these early childish fear thoughts, guilt complexes, and frustrations with them into adult life. We go about our daily experiences with our subconscious mind crammed full of negative complexes, and wonder why life is such a failure, why our health is bad, why we have no peace of mind, and why the world seems to be against us.

It is my hope that somewhere in this text some may find a key which can be used to "tune in" to the power, the love and the abundance of God's good, which is the divine heritage of every man and woman on earth.

—LAWRENCE HINCKLEY

A NEW CONCEPT

I remember a sentence I read in a little book or magazine some years ago. It was, *"God loves me, and approves of me!"* I will never forget the first time I read this. It shocked me! It even sounded sacrilegious. Most of my life I had lived with the idea that I was a sinner, and such a miserable one, God couldn't possibly think well of me, let alone *approve* of me. So the above statement was a stunning revelation. I kept thinking about it; "God loves me, and approves of me!" I found myself saying it over and over many times a day. My very acceptance of His approval of me seemed to give me strength and understanding and a deep desire to do only that which was acceptable and worthy in His sight.

I did not realize it at the time, but now I know that this sentence was the key which opened up a new concept of God for me. It changed my life. God was no longer the austere king, nor was He afar off. He was a loving "Father" who was close to me, who loved me and *approved* of me! I became enthusiastic about my work because I knew that *God* was interested.

It was at this point that many things started to happen in my life experience — good things. I found new interests and a new vitality. Among other things, business picked up, my health improved, and love began to replace cynicism. I liked this feeling of one-ness with life. It was as though some heavy burden had been cast aside. For the first time in my adult life I began to experience the joy of living and thanking God for every minute of the day.

As a child I attended Sunday school and as an adult I often attended church. I confess, however, that my attendance ebbed and flowed with the tide. Although I had many years' exposure to God's message, it just didn't penetrate through my rather negative attitude toward life. This was due in part to the fact that many of the good men who gave it, although very dedicated and sincere, used just as negative an approach in delivering God's message as I used in receiving it. I often came away from the sermon in a depressed mood. It was wonderful, therefore, to have such a joyous revelation of an approving God.

A NEW CONCEPT

You may well ask, "How could God approve of me if I were a thief, or a murderer, or had a nasty disposition, etc.?" God certainly does not approve of the acts of thievery or murder or cruelty. However, when the criminal turns to God for guidance, he ceases to be a thief, or a murderer. There are thousands of cases where former criminals have attuned their lives to God, and have led happy and normal lives thereafter. Your *acceptance* of the fact that God is interested in you brings you in closer communion with Him. This acceptance alone can change your life.

I started reading other books devoted to this line of thought. I have since studied the Bible, religious history, comparative religions, books on religious philosophy, and especially the New Testament. Of the many books I read, the New Testament seemed to contain the information I needed most. Jesus' concept of God and the truths to be found in His teachings are as applicable today as they were in the lives of those people two thousand years ago.

I SCAN EARLY RELIGIONS

My studies took me far back beyond the time of
Jesus, back to man's earliest ideas about God. It
is said that never in history has there been any tribe
of men (even the most primitive savages) who
haven't had a belief in a Supreme Being or some
sort of God. They also believed in some form of
after-life.

In the first place primitive man was in fear and
awe of all mysteries of nature which he did not
understand. He realized that there was a power in
the world greater than himself and his fellows.
These primitive people feared the storm, the light-
ning, the rain, the thunder. When the fury of the
elements descended upon them, they thought they
had done something to provoke the anger of the
storm, and they were afraid.

And so it developed that these early tribes began
to believe that there was a god in the storm; a god
in the wind; a god in the sun; a god who took away
their people at his will.

Thus it was that early religion was based on *fear*,

fear of superior beings or forces which the people did not understand.

Next began the practice of giving sacrifices to these gods to appease and placate their anger. When gentle rains fell and watered the crops, the people were happy. They felt the storm god was pleased with them. In the very first concepts of God, these early tribes had the combination of a god of wrath and a god of love. One who punished them when they displeased him and blessed them when they appeared good in his sight.

There are of course many religions throughout the world, in addition to our Christian religion. Perhaps the earliest of these was Hinduism. Its followers believe that Hinduism dates back 4,000 years, and that it is the fountainhead of all other religions. In some of their early writings, we find an interesting concept of one God, who was the whole universe, and yet could be found in the innermost self. These early writings are both beautiful and inspiring.

Moses is credited with the first writings of the Old Testament on which Judaism is based. Christianity of course dates from the time of Jesus, nearly 2,000 years ago.

Buddha is another leader whose teachings spread to China, Tibet, Japan, and many other countries.

Mohammedanism was founded about 612 A.D., and is one of the youngest of all the great religions.

Confucius was primarily a teacher of ethics.

These are some of the most widely known religions of the world.

In reading the Old Testament of our Bible, we find that the concept of God (usually referred to as Jehovah) was, for the most part, that of a super-king. His was the rule of "an eye for an eye, and a tooth for a tooth."

It is interesting to compare this conception with that of early man's first idea of a god who was a god of wrath one minute and a god of love the next. One who blessed His people when they appeared good in His sight and punished them when they displeased Him. The Old Testament Jehovah was usually depicted as a stern king who said, "Thou shalt *not* do this, and thou shalt *not* do that."

Primitive man based his religion on fear, and in the Old Testament times, God was feared in much the same way. People worshipped and obeyed primarily because of *fear*. They offered sacrifices (even human sacrifices) to appease Him.

Then came the Master, Jesus, "the Light of the World," with an absolutely revolutionary teaching. His teaching was of God as our "loving Father." A God of *love* in whom we live and move and have our being. One who is "nearer than breathing and closer than hands and feet!" Jesus replaced the Old Testament God of an eye for an eye and a tooth for a tooth, with a God of love. He replaced the old concept of *fear* with one of *love* and God's eternal goodness. The keynote of all Jesus' teaching was LOVE and forgiveness.

Jesus said, "Fear not little flock, for it is your Father's good pleasure to give you the kingdom. Let not your heart be troubled, neither let it be afraid." He taught that we are all children of God and one with the Almighty. He gave us three new commandments. Two of these commandments are to love God and to love our neighbor! And He said that on these two "hang all the Law and the Prophets." His third and last commandment was to "love one another as I have loved you."

The Bible states, "Love overcometh all things, love never faileth." "There is no fear in love; but perfect love casteth out fear."

Jesus didn't frighten His people into a knowledge

of God. He said that as human parents we were conscious of how much we loved our children; and knowing this, how much greater then was the love of our Creator for *His* children.

And who are His children? You and I and our neighbors across the sea. "(God) hath made of one blood all nations of men." (Acts 17:26) We are all His children.

In the parable of the prodigal son, Jesus tells of the son who left his father's house, to lead a life of sin. When he returned again to his father's house, did the father rebuke him in any way? No indeed, he welcomed him with all his LOVE and gave him suitable raiment and prepared a feast in his honor.

During the time of Jesus' teaching, he practiced this parable. He said to those who had sinned and came to Him for help, "Go and sin no more." If they needed physical help, He healed their bodies! Instead of condemnation or rebuke, He gave them love and hope and life.

I would like to take the time right here to give a few quotations from the Bible. These are not passages that need interpreting, but state the truth in plain and simple language. If we read and believe, they are a wonderful source of inspiration and instruction.

God is love. I John 4:16

The Lord is good. Ps. 100:5

The earth is full of the goodness of the Lord. Ps. 33:5

All things work together for good to them that love God. Rom. 8:28

For thou, Lord, art good, and ready to forgive; and plenteous in mercy unto all them that call upon thee. Ps. 86:5

Whoso trusteth in the Lord, happy is he. Prov. 16:20

If we love one another, God dwelleth in us, and His love is perfected in us. I John 4:12

He that dwelleth in love dwelleth in God, and God in him. I John 4:16

Rejoice in the Lord always. Phil. 4:4

These are plain statements that the Lord is good and that the earth is full of His goodness; that God dwells within us and that we should love Him and love one another. We should rejoice, trust in God, and be happy.

Some might argue that one can prove anything by the Bible. It is true that passages may be twisted in their interpretation to cover almost any situation;

but it is pretty hard to twist the statements given above. They are straightforward, simple truths. If people would just believe and live these few passages, the problems of this world would be solved. There would be happiness, plenty, love and peace.

"SIN"

As this word "sin" seems so important in religious teachings, let us find out just what it means. The first thing we find is that the various denominations have different ideas as to just what is sinful and what isn't. This makes a very confused picture.

It is said the word sin is derived from an ancient word which meant missing the mark when using the bow and arrow. Thus when we sin, we miss the mark or make a mistake. Most modern dictionaries define sin as breaking a religious or moral law.

There are many laws in the law books of our country, and in foreign countries we find still different laws. What is lawful in one state might be unlawful in another.

What is true regarding civil laws is also true of religious laws. And speaking of religious laws, did you know that when Jesus was teaching, the church had 600 laws for the Sabbath day alone? And Jesus was continually being criticized for breaking some of these laws, or sinning!

Jesus ignored the hundreds of unimportant edicts

and substituted a few simple laws which are as applicable today as they were in His time, because they are based on eternal truth. An example is Jesus' teaching; "Thou shalt love the Lord thy God with all thy heart, and with all thy soul, and with all thy mind, and with all thy strength; and this is the first commandment. And the second is like, namely, Thou shalt love thy neighbor as thyself. There is none other commandment greater than these."

Some religious groups consider it a sin for people to dance. To some denominations it is a sin to wear a bathing suit. Some consider it sinful to play cards. Others say it is wrong to have a picnic on the Sabbath day. Some churches do not allow singing! Some say we should attend church on Saturday, and assure us that it is all right to carry on our business on Sunday; while others reverse this and say it is a sin to work on Sunday, but it is all right for us to work on Saturday! No wonder people get confused!

Not long ago I came upon another definition of sin. It is a wonderful concept; it straightens out all this confusion like a light in the dark. It is this: "Sin is anything we do that tends to harm body or mind, or do harm in any way to any other person, or mistreat any living creature." Think about this, and see how close it comes to the teachings of the Master.

To carry this thought one step further, we are told by eminent physicians that fear, worry, frustration and guilt feelings harm the body and mind. Therefore we should consider these to be "sins" as well.

CHURCHES SERVE MAN

The churches of this country and throughout the world do a wonderful service for mankind. The fact that there are many sects and denominations may seem puzzling to some of us. We know that every person on this earth was created by God, for man cannot create life. Thus it can be said we are all children of God, but here is the interesting point: God never created two people exactly alike. Each of us is an individual with free will and choice. The fact that there are many churches and beliefs is a wonderful thing. It is possible in this way for every person to find a church or religious belief that gives him the spiritual food he needs. Every man has the right to worship as he pleases and in the church of his choice. All are worshipping the same God.

The mistake made, however, is when one group or organization or denomination claims that its way is the ONLY way, and that anyone who does not go down this specific path is a doomed soul. This holds true on a world scale with the various religions, as well as on the small scale of various churches within a community. God does *not* love one church or one religious group or one people more than any other, any more than He loves the white man more than the black.

There is only one God. This one God created the universe and everything in it. This one God loves us all and "If we love one another, God dwelleth in us, and His love is perfected in us."

Science and religion used to be worlds apart; now they find no real basis for conflict upon any of the great truths Jesus taught so many years ago.

Although some say that today is a new era in religion and religious belief, it is simply going back and studying with an open mind the *teachings* of Jesus and His teaching of God as a loving Father; a God who is willing and able to help us live NOW; who solves our daily problems; who heals us of our sickness; a God to whom we can go in any emergency with complete and absolute faith that before we call He will answer and while we are yet speaking He will hear; and whatsoever we ask, *believing*, we shall receive. The manner or form in which we go to God in a prayer is not important. It doesn't matter whether we are in a church or on the street. God is everywhere present and is with us every second of the day and night. "In Him we live and move and have our being." It is a wonderful feeling, this being at one with God; feeling His closeness (closer than hands and feet), and responding to His eternal love. Of knowing that you are important in His sight, that He loves you and APPROVES of you.

"AS A MAN THINKETH"

You may recall that Paul said, "Whatsoever things are true, whatsoever things are honest, whatsoever things are just, whatsoever things are pure, whatsoever things are lovely, whatsoever things are of good report; if there be any virtue, and if there be any praise, think on these things." How many of us who profess to be Christians would allow the world to know every thought we let go through our minds in twenty-four hours? How about just ONE hour? Many people seem to think that our thoughts and our religion have no connection.

The Bible says, "for as a man thinketh in his heart, so is he." In other words, let your thoughts dwell on sickness, poverty, failure, worry, etc., and you stand a very good chance of bringing these negative conditions into your life and experience. My own years as an expert "worrier" brought them all. I demonstrated this law to perfection. An eminent M.D. said to me, not long ago, that worry, guilt complexes, frustration and negative thinking have brought on either mental illness or real physical disorders in fully 80% of the patients who come to his office.

Paul knew the value of right thinking; and to separate our religion and our thought is like separating the head from the rest of the body. If a man *is* what he thinks in his heart, then he should think things that are lovely, things that are of good report. To be successful he should THINK success, to bring love into his life, he must THINK love; love for his neighbor, love for his enemy, love for the world, and God will answer by surrounding him with love, for affirmative thought is a powerful prayer for good.

When you meet a friend in the street and tell her of your aches, pains, and troubles; and she responds with a lurid account of her husband's operation and a detailed report on everything the surgeon removed, and then the two of you try to outdo each other telling the sordid details of a recent automobile wreck, are your minds on "things of good report," or "whatsoever things are lovely"?

Possibly this conversation is followed by some vicious local scandal. Does this sort of thinking coincide with Jesus' teaching of "love thy neighbor"? In I Peter 3:10 we read, "He that would love life, and see good days, let him refrain his tongue from evil, and his lips that they speak no guile." In Proverbs 18:7 we read, "A fool's mouth is his destruction, and his lips are the snare of his soul."

When you think of aches and pains, troubles and sorrows, scandal and filth, you are planting these thoughts deep in your OWN mind. If pains, troubles, sorrows, and scandal appear in your life, you should know where they came from; for "as a man thinketh in his heart, so is he."

THOUGHTS COME FIRST

Did it ever occur to you that everything comes from a thought? Look about you in your home; the television set, the floor furnace with its automatic control, the vacuum cleaner. Before any one of these could be manufactured, someone had to THINK and visualize it in his mind. *Everything* is first a *thought*. Next a PATTERN is made. After the pattern is formed, the article can be manufactured into a visual tangible object. First the mind, or thought, then the forming of the pattern, then the objectification of what the mind has conceived.

In our lives it is the same idea all over again. Think poverty long enough to form the pattern, and you are apt to bring it into actuality; the same goes for other negative thought patterns.

I'm afraid the person who says, "What do my thoughts have to do with my religion?", isn't thinking very deeply. Too many of us divorce our religion from our everyday lives, from our business, *from our everyday thoughts;* and yet God is with us every second of every day.

THOUGHTS COME FIRST

If you are experiencing things in your life which you do not like, why not try this experiment? It will surely do no harm. Try changing your thought pattern to better things. You must think these thoughts "in your heart" and have a real belief in them. Jesus told us that it will be done unto us as we believe. If you are sincere, the pattern will change. Just wishful thinking will do no good. You must be sincere. I know that in my own case, the change from negative to positive thinking changed the pattern of my life. As I made a new pattern of joy, love, health, and abundance, I began to experience many of these God-given blessings just as easily as I formerly demonstrated frustration and failure. It didn't all come about at once, and I still have a long way to go. I do not set myself up as an example. It is hard to erase the effects of many years of negation overnight. But if we keep working at it, we will come to know happiness beyond our fondest dreams. "Whatsoever things are lovely, whatsoever things are of good report, . . . think on these things."

We all know how negative thoughts affect us. We have heard how sudden fear can turn the hair white overnight; how worry and guilt complexes can actually bring on serious illness; how a telegram with news of a negative nature will cause the heart to beat so fast that it almost runs away with itself, whether the news is true or false. The shock might even cause some people to faint dead away. And yet these reactions are *all* caused by our thoughts. Couldn't it be just as true then, that reversing these negative thoughts to positive ones might bring calmness in place of panic, health in place of sickness, joy in place of sorrow, and put faith and love in our hearts in place of fear? It is surely worth a try.

When we turn our thoughts toward God's love, and start giving thanks for our blessings instead of bemoaning our lack, we soon find ourselves tuned in to the power and strength and goodness of God. No one on earth could convince me that God hasn't given me love and help every day since that eventful moment when I truly accepted Jesus' teaching of God as a loving father, a Father who *approves* of me. My problem of making a career in my chosen profession has been solved. I am surrounded by a loving family and am blessed with many friends. Best of all, I feel a closer union with God.

"LOVE GOD"

There may be some who are puzzled over the fact that Jesus said we should "love God with all our mind and with all our heart," and at the same time there are places in the Bible where it says to fear God. Knowing that it is impossible to love anyone with all my heart and at the same time to be in fear of him, I decided to look up the word fear and see if it meant anything other than a sense of fright or terror. I found that in reading these Bible passages I could substitute the word "respect" for the word fear, and it seemed to fit perfectly. So it was with great interest that I found, among others, this definition, "Fear: to regard with reverence and awe." When we use this definition in place of the word "fear," we get a far different interpretation. Many times the Bible uses the words fear and awe together. As love and fear (when we use it in the sense of being afraid) are at the opposite ends of the pole, as love is positive and fear is in this sense negative, it is no wonder that the phrase "fear God" might be puzzling if we give it this negative interpretation.

However, Jesus is forceful in His commandment to *love* God, and in His concept of God as our loving Father. Also in so many of His statements such as: "Fear not little flock, for it is your Father's good pleasure to give you the kingdom." and many, many others. We need only to believe Jesus and not let our heart be troubled, neither let it be *afraid*.

It is true that when we think of the power of God, which is the power of the universe, we are awed by His omnipotence. And yet this same God-power is with us and within us to help solve any and all of our problems and for this we should give a prayer of thanks without ceasing. The more we learn about God and His love and His power and His eternal goodness, the happier and richer our lives become. "For I, the Lord thy God, will hold thy right hand saying unto thee, 'Fear not, I will help thee' " (Isaiah 41:13). Do not be afraid of life, and do not be afraid of death. Fear, in its negative sense is our worst enemy. Replace fear with trust and faith, and your world will change from worry and frustration to joy and peace of mind in the twinkling of an eye!

DO YOU LOVE YOUR NEIGHBOR?

Carry out the commandments which Jesus said were so important; love God with all your heart, and love your neighbor. I have never known anyone with real love for God and his fellow man to be a pessimist.

Some people say, "Suppose my neighbor is a gangster, or a man with a hateful disposition, or a drunkard. How would I love that kind of a neighbor?" This question is a fair one and as always Jesus gives us the answer. In the first place He said, "Love your enemies." If it is possible to love an enemy, it must be possible to love your neighbor no matter what his shortcomings may be.

But how can anyone love an enemy? It is true that this sounds like an impossible edict. We must first understand that Jesus had insight into the Truth. He was never fooled by any outward appearance, no matter how negative it appeared to be on the surface. If anyone came to Him to be healed of a disease, He paid no attention to the outward appearance. It made no difference to Him whether this person had been ill for ten days or ten years; whether he was crippled or blind or had cancer or any other negative condition. Jesus saw only the whole, perfect man he REALLY was; the God-like qualities, the child of God, with God's health and God's perfection — and Jesus would accept nothing less. He told us not to judge by outward appearance, but to judge righteous judgment. He looked under the veneer of appearance to the spiritual man beneath.

To come back to our neighbor who is hateful, dishonest, etc. We do not have to love these *qualities* about him. Jesus would not expect us to do this. We must look beneath the surface at the man he would be, the child of God, and love the REAL neighbor and not the ugly, ill-appearing crust he has formed through years of negative thinking and living. We are *all* children of God, which means that we have the wonderful qualities of God within us. The qualities of love, health, goodness, joy, peace, abundance, happiness. The fact that at the moment we are outwardly expressing hate, sickness, sorrow and dishonesty does not alter this fact! The Bible assures us that love overcometh all things, and that it never fails. So love your neighbor for what you know him to *really* be, and overlook his cantankerous outward expression, and maybe you will melt some of that crust of unpleasantness away and let a little of God's goodness show through!

There are also times when you may have a wonderful neighbor living next door, and you still find it hard to love him. Envy and jealousy often enter the picture. I recall a fine man who lived next door to me for several years. He kept his hedge and lawn looking like a park. All his flowers grew larger and more beautiful than mine. He spent hours keeping the fallen leaves raked meticulously from his well-mowed lawn. His picket fence was always freshly painted. By comparison my yard looked shockingly unkempt. And did I have the proper love and respect for him? I must confess that I did not. In fact his virtues irritated me no end!

What of the neighbor who seems to have everything you lack? All his investments prove to be gold mines; and he is always buying a new car, or boat, or perhaps mink for his wife. Do you really feel happy for him, or must you confess a few jealous pangs?

And you women; what about the beautiful woman next door who always keeps her house immaculate and her five children neat as a pin? She is also a wonderful cook, president of the woman's club, active in the Brownies and Scouts, and a completely charming person. Do you feel a slight twinge of envy?

Although it sounds amusing to tell of these things, this is a more serious subject than would appear on the surface. Our thoughts of envy and irritation should be replaced by genuine admiration and love for the admirable qualities and skills of our good friends next door, and to carry it further, our neighbors across the sea.

We wonder why there is not a true feeling of peace and good will throughout the world today, and we find this same situation; this sort of envy, jealousy, and ill feeling on a national and international scale sows the seeds of war and destruction.

THIS WONDERFUL BODY OF OURS

Jesus also said, "The kingdom of God is within you." And where is "within you"? It obviously isn't far off in the sky somewhere, or over the next hill, or on the other side of the globe. If this had been the case, Jesus would have said so. He said "within you." Many of us miss the wonder of the great Master's teaching because of its very simplicity. We build up all sorts of theories about what He may have meant, instead of just believing His words.

Paul referred to our body as the temple of the living God, and just a little thought about it will show us why. Do you really appreciate this most marvelous of all of God's creations? Have you ever taken the time to thank God for your body? And lastly, have you ever felt any real connection between your religion and your body? In the first place, it is the most wonderful mechanism in the world. All of man's greatest inventions are child's play in comparison. The nerves flashing messages to the brain, parts of the body continually renewing themselves (casting off the old and building the new), constant healing (cut your finger and watch God's healing power go to work). It isn't *your* healing power, for as smart as you are, you don't even know a tiny part of all the wonderful things that happen in your body when you do such a simple thing as to cut your finger. A learned physician could write a whole book on this subject alone! I mention this to show that God never creates anything and then leaves it to shift for itself. You may think you are extremely intelligent, — but can you make your own heart beat? You cannot do that any more than you can change the food you eat into bone, muscles, and skin.

When Paul said, "In Him we live and move and have our being," he meant just what he said. How could it be otherwise, with the Spirit of God actually with us and within us every second of the day and night, taking care of His creation. Ask any physician if he could heal our wounds, were it not for a divine healing force which pours through our bodies constantly. The surgeon can cut us open, *sew* up the wound, but *he* cannot *heal* it. Whose power is it that keeps your heart beating? I do not see how any thinking person can refute the fact that there is a Power in this universe greater than himself. Thus we realize that the power of God is actually within us and helping us every second!

JUST WHAT IS SPIRIT?

Jesus also said, "God is Spirit, (some versions give 'a Spirit') and he that worships Him must worship Him in Spirit and in Truth." As Jesus defined God as Spirit, I decided the best thing to do was to look up the word "spirit," and I found some very interesting definitions. I found that "Spirit is life or intelligence conceived of entirely apart from physical embodiment. It is vital essence, force, energy, as distinct from matter." Also given were such definitions as "Life, God, the Life Principle, a Divine animating influence."

As we have found, it takes intelligence or thought to create the simplest little device. Then a pattern is made, and finally the actual creating of the visual object. As God is Spirit, He is therefore the creating intelligence and life force, or energy, back of all visual things.

To understand this better, let us take another look at this body of ours. Have you ever bumped your shin against a box, a chair leg, or a bed post? If you have, you probably would be willing to bet anyone that your body is a solid object. Yet science tells us a different story. Suppose I asked you what your body is composed of. You might answer, "hands, feet, head, torso, etc." Maybe that is all the thought many of us give to it. But if we continue to reduce our bodies into component parts, we come to the realization that we are made up of billions of tiny cells. These tiny cells are made up of molecules and the molecules in turn are made up of atoms. Scientists are discovering more about the atom daily. I have read that atoms are composed of protons, electrons and neutrons, in constant motion and with spaces between them comparable in relation to their size to the distances between the earth, the sun, the planets, and the stars! Thus we find that our bodies are actually made up of the motion and energy of the universe, the power and energy of God! And so we find that God, Creator of the universe, has actually made our bodies of the same life force, energy, or universal substance of which everything in the universe is made.

This oneness with all of God's creation is a wonderful thought. The trees, the rocks, the flowers, the stream, everything about us is actually made of the same universal substance that our bodies are made of, only differing in their atomic structure (in number and arrangement of electrons, neutrons, and protons). Now we can see how it would be impossible for a sparrow to fall without God's knowledge of it, for God as Spirit is everywhere!

Remember, it was Jesus who gave us the concept of God as Spirit. Today we find science and religion closer in their views than at any time in the world's history. The late Albert Einstein gave us an equation which in effect means that energy and mass are identical and interchangeable. This seems to be just another way of saying that God's Spirit is everywhere and we are one with Spirit.

"I AM"

In the studies of the many religions of the world and in the various denominations which make up our Christian religion, we find a number of names given for God. Any and all of them refer to the same God. The Old Testament often spoke of Jehovah. Some refer to God as The Creator, Supreme Being, or Emmanuel. Then there is The Deity, and Lord. In some metaphysical churches, they refer to God as Principle, First Cause, or the Thing Itself.

Due to my early orthodox training, I use the word God. No other word seems to be quite as strong, so far as I personally am concerned, when referring to the power which is greater than we are, the power which governs the universe.

In the Old Testament there is still another name. If you are a student of the Bible, you will remember that this was the name God told Moses to use. When Moses was called by God to lead the children of Israel out of Egypt, this great man said unto God, "Behold, when I come unto the children of Israel and shall say unto them, 'The God of your fathers hath sent me unto you'; and they shall say to me, 'What is His name?' What shall I say unto them?"

And God said unto Moses, "I AM THAT I AM." And He said, "Thus shalt thou say unto the children of Israel, I AM hath sent me unto you." And God said moreover unto Moses, "Thus shalt thou say unto the children of Israel, 'The Lord God of your fathers, the God of Abraham, the God of Isaac, and the God of Jacob, hath sent me unto you: this *is* my name forever, and this *is* my memorial unto all generations!" (Exodus 3:13-15) Thus we find that the Bible gives "I AM" as another name for God, or for God's power and authority. It also states that this is God's name forever, even unto all generations.

The above writings in Exodus give us a very interesting thought. There is no stronger statement in our language than the use of the two words "I AM" in a sentence. For instance when you say, "*I am* well, *I am* strong, *I am* happy," you use these words to express your feelings in the strongest possible way. There is power in the use of these two words no matter what thought we express with them. As God gave "I AM" as His name and His authority for all generations, isn't it logical to suppose that the statement "I AM" carries God's power today just as it did in the days of Moses? If this is the case, when we say "I am healthy, I am loved, I am joyful," we are not only affirming these facts in a positive way, but we are actually giving an affirmative prayer. In our Bible in Job we read, "Decree a thing and it shall be established unto thee." We are praying for health, love, and joy to be expressed in our lives, and we are giving this prayer the power and authority of God.

On the other hand, when we say, "I am sick, I am tired, I am unhappy," we are using the full power of the universe to bring about these negative conditions. I know that I shall be very careful how I use the words "I AM" in the future. They may be more important to my happiness than I have ever realized.

WHERE TO FIND GOD

With the concept of God as everywhere present, in all and through all; a God in whom we live and move and have our being; a God who is not just powerful but all the power there is in the universe; a God who is not just a God of love, but all the love in the world; a God who is not simply good, but all the good there is in the world; how is it possible for any of us to go through life feeling alone or unloved?

I once heard a minister give this statement, "To say you can't find God is like a fish looking for the water it is swimming in." In God we live and move and have our being, and yet some of us say we can't find Him. The Bible says that God fills all space. "Do not I fill heaven and earth?" If God is omnipresent, then where can we go and not find Him? It sounds silly to think of a fish swimming around looking for water, and it is equally silly for men to say they can't find God.

Look at a mother tenderly holding her baby, and you see God expressing as love through this mother.

WHERE TO FIND GOD

When you see someone take a blind man by the arm and lead him safely across a busy street, you see the kindness of God expressed by this good Samaritan. When you see a flower opening in all its colorful glory, you see God expressing as beauty through the medium of this flower.

If you cannot find God, you simply do not want to find Him! Jesus gave us a statement that applies to people who cannot find God. "Hearing ye shall hear, and shall not understand; and seeing ye shall see, and shall not perceive: For this people's heart is waxed gross, and their ears are dull of hearing, and their eyes they have closed." Jesus also said, "Seek and ye shall find, knock and it shall be opened unto you." So if we truly seek God we will find Him — not afar off, but right where we are at this very moment.

IS IT SAINTLY TO BE POOR?

Some religious groups think it is more saintly to be poor than to be rich. This idea stems from a statement Jesus made about how hard it was for a rich man to enter into the Kingdom of Heaven. At the time of Jesus' teaching, there were two classes of people, the very rich and the very poor. There was no middle class as we know it today. The vast majority of the very well-to-do people had attained this wealth by taking undue advantage of the poor.

There was yet another reason for Jesus' statement. It holds as true today as it did in Jesus' time, and it is that many people get so attached to wealth and possessions that they make the attainment of material "things" the goal of their lives. In other words, they worship *possessions* instead of God. You recall the Bible story of the rich young man who was so attached to his property and earthly possessions that he could not give them up and follow Jesus?

When the attainment of gold, or buildings, or land, or houses becomes the ultimate goal of anyone, then riches can rightly be termed a sin. The first commandment is, "Thou shalt have no other gods before Me." When man makes a god out of possessions or any "thing," he violates the primary commandment. When we hurt anyone in any way in the attainment of possessions, by any unfair dealings, we will find it hard to enter the Kingdom. There are many people who go to church on Sunday, and yet find it easy to take unfair advantage of some poor widow in a business deal on Monday. I am sure such people would be surprised to be told they had done anything wrong. They would say, "It was a legitimate business deal." They completely divorce their business from their religion, and see no connecting link between.

Jesus knew of the abundance of God and His willingness to give all things to His children. So it is not *riches*, but our attitude that is important. It is right that we should have abundance of all good things in this life, providing we do not make the *accumulation* of them our consuming interest (our God), or providing we harm no one either directly or indirectly in attaining these "things." It is not a sin to drive a fine car, or to own a thriving business or farm.

BRIDGE TO A BETTER LIFE

There is nothing wrong in buying an automatic washing machine to lessen the drudgery of life, or to equip the kitchen of your home with the very latest in automatic dish-washers, a deep freeze, a fine range, etc.

God's supply is unlimited, and He does not stint anyone. "Ask and it shall be given unto you." It is just as saintly to live in the finest house in town as to live in a shanty. In fact God intends the best for His children. Jesus said, "I am come that ye might have life, and have it more *abundantly*."

Look about you and you will see nature's lavish abundance everywhere. Pray for the things you need. Your Father knows what things you have need of, even before you pray! If you have the right attitude about wealth, it can never make you a sinner or lower your chances of entering the Kingdom. "If they hearken and serve Him, they shall spend their days in prosperity and their years in pleasantness." (Job 36:11 E.R.V.) "Delight thyself also in the Lord, and He shall give thee the desires of thine heart." (Psalms 37:4)

There is a saying that I have often heard and I think it is a wonderful thought. "The best of myself for the world, and the best of the world for myself." Refuse to be bound by the thought that poverty and Godliness go hand in hand. Seek God first, and then these things shall be added unto you. "They that seek the Lord shall not want any good thing." (Psalms 34:10)

But we must seek God *first*, and make the accumulation of "things" of a secondary nature. When we think more of *giving* and less of *getting*, we take a big step forward in learning the secret of a happy life. It is well said that it is not what we "take up" but what we "give up" in this life that makes us rich.

ARE THE WEALTHY HAPPY?

I think all of us know a few wealthy people. Possibly some of us have attained great wealth. In my own experience as an artist, I have met many who have achieved great wealth. Now, if money were the answer to happiness, if it were the most important attainment on this earth, these people should be happy. They should have peace of mind and joy in their daily lives; and yet these people of wealth seem not a bit happier than those who work for them. So it is obvious that money doesn't bring true happiness; but poverty isn't the answer either, for it brings neither happiness nor peace of mind.

Thus we are forced to conclude that it is something besides the attainment of earthly possessions that brings us what we need most in this life.

It isn't fame, for we all know of frustrated movie stars with their many divorces and law suits and contract bickering and nervous tensions.

It isn't even health, for all of us know many individuals with healthy bodies who spend most of their waking moments complaining.

There are some who might claim that we make no headway until we meet adversity. As I stated before, it doesn't seem to be *what* conditions we encounter, good or bad, that is so important. *The important thing is how we meet them.* If it is a negative condition that faces us, it is how we meet it and rise above it. It is HOW we live each day, and I find no better way than to live by the rules given to us by Jesus. Love God, love our neighbor as ourselves, have a true faith in the goodness and mercy of God, and keep right on believing, no matter how dark the outer picture may sometimes look.

I believe it is when we do for others, forgetting ourselves, and our own selfish desires, that the greatest happiness comes our way. Jesus said, "Love one another as I have loved you." This means without any thought of selfish reward.

SANCTIMONIOUSNESS

Along with the idea that it is sinful to be rich, is another idea that has always been puzzling to me. It is the idea that extreme solemnity and sanctimoniousness are more Godly than expressions of joy. Jesus said, "And these things I speak in the world, that they might have my joy fulfilled in themselves." "These things have I spoken unto you that my joy might remain in you, and that your joy might be full." In our Bible we read, "Be glad in the Lord, and rejoice, ye righteous; and shout for joy, all that are upright in heart. . . . Be ye glad and rejoice forever in that which I create. . . . Ye shall rejoice in all that ye put your hand unto. . . . Thou hast put gladness in my heart. . . . He is not a God of the dead, but of the living."

And so it goes; I could quote on and on. God did not put us here and give us life and then consider it more to His liking for us to spend that life in sorrow and negation than in thanksgiving, in happiness, in praise, and in joy. Nothing should make us happier than our religion, our feeling of oneness with our Father. It should fill our cup to overflow-ing every day. "Whoso trusteth in the Lord, happy is he." (Proverbs 16:20)

OUR FATHER

Jesus not only gave the world the idea of God as a loving Father, but He gave us a prayer which is used in Christian churches throughout the world. It is as applicable today as it was almost two thousand years ago. He starts with the two words upon which He bases His whole concept of God: "OUR FATHER"—not just MY Father, but OUR Father. Father to ALL men; black, white, yellow, or brown. God is "Our Father."

"Which art in Heaven" — whether Heaven is thought of as a place or a state of mind, it symbolizes only good. It is joy, perfect health, peace of mind, strength, unselfish love, unlimited good, supreme happiness! God is one with all these things. It is another way of saying what Jesus said again and again in His teachings, that God is good, and that God is love.

"Hallowed be Thy name" — as we know, God told Moses His name, and gave His name as "I AM." As these words are associated with God and Heaven, they are associated only with good, and never with evil or anything negative.

"Thy Kingdom come, Thy will be done in earth as it is in Heaven" — Jesus said the Kingdom of God is within us, so the closer we attune our lives to God, the more it will bring Heaven (or all the good which God has for His children) into our everyday lives. Peace of mind, joy, health, love, unlimited good can indeed transform our everyday living into a Heaven on earth!

"Give us this day our daily bread" — bread in this instance means not only our daily food and material needs, but means also that we need to partake of spiritual bread.

"And forgive us our debts as we forgive our debtors" — Jesus said many times that we MUST forgive. If we have any feeling of envy, hate, jealousy, or condemnation toward anyone, we must *forgive*. We must also forgive *ourselves* and hold no thought of distrust or condemnation or guilt. We must forgive.

"Lead us not into temptation, but deliver us from evil." The closer we are led to God, the less power will any temptation or evil have over us. When we are spiritually in tune with God, all evil and negative appearances disappear from our lives as darkness goes when we turn on the light.

"For Thine is the kingdom, and the power, and the glory forever" — kingdom is the realm of God or the expression of God, and the kingdom of God is within us. The power of God is omnipotent and the glory or the action of God is everywhere and forever. As we express more of God, we express more of the goodness, the power, and the love of the Almighty in our lives today!

LIGHT

Has it ever occurred to you that light is also important to think about when we contemplate our religious philosophy? To quote from our Bible, "God is light, and in Him is no darkness at all." Just what does this mean? The Bible gives us one answer when it refers to light as good, and darkness as evil. Thus transposing the words light, and darkness, to good and evil we have "God is good, and in Him is no evil at all."

Jesus said, "I am the light of the world; he that followeth Me shall not walk in darkness, but shall have the light of life." He also said, "I am come a light into the world, that whosoever believeth on Me should not abide in darkness." From the above statements we find that He referred to light as spiritual understanding and darkness as ignorance or lack of knowledge. We can then refer to God as knowledge (all knowledge) and darkness as lack of knowledge.

In I Thess. 5:5 we read, "Ye are all children of light, and children of the day; we are not of the night nor of the darkness." Have you ever seen a person's face light up with joy? You have heard the expression of how a happy person's eyes shine. Light is always associated with goodness, with knowledge, with happiness, with joy, throughout the Bible. "Let your light so shine." This gives us still further proof, if further proof is needed, that God is good; God is supreme knowledge; God is joy, happiness and love! In Him is no darkness, no ignorance, no sorrow, nothing negative.

There is actual power in light, but none in darkness. To illustrate, take a flashlight and go into a dark room. One flash of your light and it pierces the darkness. Darkness, however, cannot pierce the light, so it is nothing but a lack of light; just as evil is a lack of good. When we have the light of understanding, the darkness, the negative and evil conditions of our world evaporate as though they had never been. As God is light and we are one with Him, it is conclusive proof that He expects OUR light to shine; expects us to be happy and live joyously NOW. When you let your light shine, it is a contagious thing, and you bring happiness and inspiration to those you contact along the way.

FEAR

Many people spend the major portion of their lives living in fear. Fear of losing a job, fear of the boss, fear about security in old age, fear of the atom rockets, fear of tornadoes, fear of losing crops, fear of loss of health!

There is a divided opinion as to how much good the numerous "health drives" do, because of our fear complexes. We hear about cancer on the television and in the newspapers, and then we worry for fear we may have it; we hear about how heart attacks take one out of every five (or some such number) persons, and we fear that we may be the next victim! We worry when there is a polio drive, etc. Fear, *fear,* FEAR!

We read about all the accidents on the road and instead of enjoying an outing in the car, we worry for fear we might have a wreck. We fear going up in a plane because it might crash.

Some people fear the dark; some fear going up in elevators, or down into caves. Some of us never advance in our work because we are afraid of change; we would rather keep the old job because we are fearful of our ability to handle the new one with its advancement in rank and pay.

And how can our religious concept help to banish fear from our lives? The answer is a simple one, but carrying it out to a successful conclusion is another matter. Our fears are deep-rooted. Many of them come from experiences of childhood and are buried deep in our subconscious minds. Fear thoughts are like poison, and yet there is one sure antidote. We must replace fear with FAITH! The Bible says, "Fear not; for I am with thee."

Have faith in God. "He shall not be afraid of evil tidings; his heart is fixed, trusting in the Lord." There are scores of such quotations. Here is one which I personally like very much: "There is no fear in love; but perfect love casteth out fear."

The more we trust in our Father, the less we fear. We do not fear the loss of our job when we have absolute faith in God's supply. We do not fear ill health when we have faith in the healing power of God. Jesus said, "Therefore I say unto you, what things soever ye desire, when ye pray, believe that ye receive them, and ye shall have them." So work to replace fear with a *positive* faith and start living your life to the fullest.

GOD'S HEALING POWER

Some may think it is God's will that we be sick; experience poverty, etc. This is similar to the fatalistic belief of many of the eastern countries.

If Jesus is right, and God is our loving Father and we in turn love Him with all our hearts, the thought that He would deliberately bring upon us sickness and suffering seems a strange thought to me. As an earthly father, did you ever sit beside the bed and listen to the breathing of a child of yours who was very ill and tossing with fever? Could you deliberately bring such a sickness upon your child? Of course you couldn't! It would be unthinkable.

Jesus said that as we who are earthly fathers like to give good things to our children, how much *more* love and goodness God is capable of giving to His chillren. Let us look at it another way. If God intends us to be sick, why is He constantly healing our wounds, building new cells in our bodies, putting His healing forces to work in the bloodstream at the first sign of trouble? There are those who might say, "Oh, you are talking about Nature. That is just Nature taking care of us." As the Bible gives God as all power, everywhere present, all in all, we might better say it is the NATURE OF GOD to heal us.

OUR ONENESS WITH GOD

I now want to use a couple of illustrations. Similar illustrations have been used by many teachers, but they both illustrate in a wonderful way our relationship and oneness with God. Let us suppose that the ocean is God and one drop of that vast ocean is yourself. You could not claim to be the whole ocean any more than you could claim to be God. You are in no sense God in His entirety, and yet all the characteristics of the ocean are also to be found in that one drop. That one drop of ocean water is truly a part of the whole, and the same elements which go to make up the ocean are to be found in that one tiny drop. So as God's nature is peace, perfection, health and joy; these wonderful Godlike qualities are also a part of you, a divine heritage. If we really believe the words of Jesus, that God is our Father, and it is inconceivable to think of God as being sick or lacking in any good thing; then why isn't it logical to suppose that we should inherit some of the characteristics of our Father. The Bible further states that God created us in His image and likeness!

BRIDGE TO A BETTER LIFE

Let us now suppose that God is a great central fountain of water. From this central fountain are hundreds and hundreds of tiny passages, each leading to some person and of course one leading to you. Through each of these tiny passages or tubes flows God's eternal goodness and mercy, His Spirit and life in a constant never-ending stream.

If you keep this passage open with a true belief in God's love, you experience God's flow of good in your life. However, God did not make man an automaton, but gave him free will and choice. The choice is yours and mine. We can give thanks for this flow of good and use it to enrich and gladden our lives and the lives of others, or we can block this passage with worry, fear, hate, frustration, or any negative block, and shut off a large portion of the good that God intends for us.

Remember, God gave you free will and choice, and if you do not experience the good things of this life, don't put the blame on God. Just take a real good look at yourself!

Suppose there are still some who say, "If God is love, joy, health, etc., and I am a part of God, how can I be sick, or think wrong thoughts, or fail in business?"

OUR ONENESS WITH GOD

Let us state still another example. I am sure you will agree that electricity is good for mankind. It does wonderful things for us all. It lights our homes, cooks our food, washes the clothes, provides power for our factories and huge industries, and aids us in a thousand ways. Electricity is found even in the very heart of the atom. It is universal God power, and God is good. And yet if we do not understand enough about it, if we are ignorant as to the laws that govern this power, it can shock us, burn us, or even electrocute us. It would be silly to blame electricity for our misfortunes.

THE POWER OF GOOD

Ignorance of the laws of electricity is no excuse and does not keep the harmful effects of its power from hurting us. The power is good and can be used in our lives for wonderful things, but if we have a wrong concept of it, throw open the wrong switch, cross the wrong wires, we suffer.

When we learn the truth about electricity, after an expert tells us how to use it, and assures us that it is good and will do wonderful things to make our lives richer and happier and fuller, we only have to believe him and carry out his instructions. Then, instead of suffering, we experience a life filled with riches of which we have never dreamed!

Jesus was this expert! He showed us how to use the laws of God. He told us how to live and receive the good that is our divine heritage.

He replaced the old law of "an eye for an eye," with love, even love of our enemies. Jesus assures us that God has only love for His children, and that we should love Him with all our hearts. We need only let the light of God's love penetrate deeply into our lives, and worry, frustration, and troubles vanish as though they had never been. We then experience the peace of mind, happiness and success that God's power and love can bring to all His children.

THE POWER OF PRAYER

If you haven't attained an absolute belief in the power of prayer, the best way to get it is *to pray*. Pray for a closer attunement to God; pray to experience a happy and successful life, pray for others. Suppose it is a health problem you need to solve; pray for perfect health. Having one prayer answered will help you more than studying one hundred books on the subject. Anyone who has prayed for a physical healing for himself or a loved one, for a new position, or for any specific and urgent need in his life and has had his prayer answered through the miracle of God's power and love, will never doubt the power of prayer again as long as he lives.

Possibly some have prayed many times, and wonder why the things they prayed for have not been forthcoming. God never refuses to answer your prayer, but is always ready to furnish your every need. In fact the Bible tells us that He knows what we have need of even before we finish our prayer. If God is not at fault, and we know He has no faults, then *we* must be to blame when the answer to our prayer does not come forth.

There are many reasons for this, and Jesus gave us one answer when He referred to the fact that when we stood praying and our brother might have aught against us, we should go to our brother, and we should *forgive*, and then we should resume our prayer.

Just what does this mean? It simply means that as long as we hold any hate or jealousy or envy or enmity of any kind against anyone (for Jesus referred to all people as brothers and sisters), we must *forgive* before we can expect God to answer our prayer.

Do you know of a single person towards whom you hold the slightest feeling of hate? Possibly this is why your prayers have gone unanswered. Cleanse your mind of this feeling, have complete forgiveness in your heart, and then go to God again in prayer.

Quarrels, antagonisms, personal hates, ill feeling, jealousies—these are some of the blocks which keep the flow of God's eternal goodness from getting through. This is also an illustration of how Love again emerges as Jesus' most important teaching. And right along with these hate thoughts we can include worry thoughts, doubt, fear, and other negatives.

Jesus stressed that we must pray BELIEVING, and you can't have an absolute belief that your prayer will be answered and have your mind filled with doubt or fear at the same time. It would be impossible. He stressed the fact many times that we must have FAITH, we must *believe* we *have* these things for which we pray, and if our belief is strong, then God's wonderful storehouse of good-will shall be opened up for us. We need only to have faith the size of a grain of mustard seed, and we can move mountains. Pray with the absolute belief you will attain that for which you have asked, and then *LET GO AND LET GOD DO THE WORK.*

Many of us pray, and then we outline to God just how He should bring these things about! If nothing seemingly happens in the first few hours or days, we start to worry and doubt that God is going to give us that for which we prayed. We pray and then say, "Now, God, snap into it and give me the answer by three o'clock tomorrow afternoon!"

When we start to worry or doubt that the answer

will be forthcoming, we have pretty well blocked our chances of getting an answer. Worry and doubt are just the reverse of FAITH and BELIEF which Jesus says are the main ingredients of a successful prayer. God works in wondrous ways His wonders to perform, so don't outline and send Him a diagram of just how to carry out your prayer. Simply trust Him and know that "All things work together for good, to them that love the Lord."

LET GO AND LET GOD

I remember one time I prayed for a particular position. I wanted this job more than any other, and it seemed right in my grasp. Then out of a clear blue sky someone else was appointed. I felt bitter about it, and could not understand why God had denied me this post. Within a month another position was given to me which was so much better that it exceeded even my fondest dreams! Had I been appointed to the first job, I would have missed out. God knew what was best for me, and answered my prayer in His own way.

I have been asked if it is necessary to ask for specific things in prayer. As we have been told, God knows our needs even before we pray, why not simply pray for God's abundant good expressed in our lives.

We are all people of free will and choice. A method that would suit me might not suit you. For some, I think this idea of praying for abundance and health and peace rather than specifying a house or a car, is a good way. In some teachings this is

76

called the absolute method of prayer. You attune yourself to God and His good, and know with absolute faith that His good is expressed in, through, and by you in every way and in everything.

If you prefer to pray for things, I feel it is better to pray for perfect transportation, rather than for a specific make and model car — it might be a lemon. Pray for a home rather than one particular house at 516 Elm Street; it might have termites. Pray for funds for your every need rather than specifying three thousand four hundred dollars; you might be limiting your good. Pray for a healthy body rather than to pray that the pain in your left epizutic be taken away. To assure that your prayer is an unselfish one, always pray that the same good be released to all mankind.

However, as stated above, we must all make up our own minds as to method; the important thing is that our prayer be unselfish and that we have an absolute faith in its fulfillment.

A QUIET TIME

It is a wonderful thing to get into the habit of setting aside a few minutes every day for a quiet time. It is best if we can find a place where we can be alone. You may remember that Jesus frequently went off by Himself to pray. If you have a comfortable chair, sit down in it and relax every muscle of your body. When you have done this, relax your mind; let go of every tension, every worry-thought, every business care, every worldly problem. Let them all drop away from you like casting off a heavy blanket which has been weighting you down. Then turn your thought to thanksgiving. You will be surprised how many things you have to be thankful for when you give the matter a little thought.

By this time you have cast off all negative thinking, all blocks, and opened the channel for God's blessings to flow through to you. In other words you have come closer to God; you truly feel your at-one-ment with God and all creation. Now pray unselfishly; send out love and good will to people of all faiths everywhere. Then ask God for any blessings you need for yourself or some loved one, and *KNOW* that He will answer your prayer. When you have finished, do not doubt or worry, just *"let go and let God."*

Do not ask for help in only the so-called disaster; let God help you with every problem of the day. Nothing is too small and nothing is too large, for with God "all things are possible."

If you get into the habit of aligning yourself with God even once during the busy day, you will be amazed how it lightens the burdens of this often hectic workaday world.

So many people today are seeking peace of mind. There is no better way to attain a feeling of peace and joy within yourself than to spend a few minutes each day just getting closer to God; realizing that health, peace, love, and happiness flow to all in a constant stream from the Divine source; that you are one with this flow of good, and that it is your divine heritage. And don't forget when you are talking to God, to be still and let Him answer you.

Tensions and worries and cares are no part of God, *therefore they are no part of you,* for we know Him to be nearer than breathing, closer than hands and feet!

LOVING OURSELVES

We hear about the Ten Commandments time and time again. They are stressed from the pulpit of churches throughout the land, but as we have stated several times, Jesus gives us *two* commandments which He tells us are of more importance than the others. "And thou shalt love the Lord thy God with all thy heart and with all thy soul, and with all thy mind, and with all thy strength; and this is the first commandment. And the second is like, namely, thou shalt love thy neighbor as thyself. There is none other commandment greater than these."

If these are such important commandments, it is just a bit puzzling as to why we hear so much about the ten and so little about these two. Just think what a wonderful world this would be if everyone kept these two! There would be no quarreling, no cheating, no robbing, no hate, no war. We should all be filled with the love of God, and love for our neighbor, and (something that many may have overlooked) LOVE FOR OURSELVES! Yes, Jesus not only says that we should have love for ourselves, but He says that this is one of the most important of the commandments. I have never heard a sermon preached on this subject.

We should love our neighbors *as ourselves*. Jesus is commanding us to love ourselves instead of depreciating ourselves, and this fact should give hope and joy and comfort to those who may have been taught to believe that self-depreciation is among the highest virtues.

The fact that Jesus stresses this commandment shows that He considers us to be children of God and as such, we should have love for ourselves as well as for our neighbors. We should love God, love our neighbors, and love *ourselves*. He does not mean arrogance or self-worship. We are all well aware that we have many faults, and that we are far from the perfection that should be our goal. We may love someone dearly and still be conscious of his or her weaknesses and faults. Jesus simply means we should have love and respect for ourselves and carry on to higher ideals and a more perfect expression of the Spirit within.

AT-ONE-MENT WITH LIFE

I realize that not only my life, but all life —
not only this world, but the whole vast universe is
governed by the same law; God's law. God's love,
His perfection, His energy, His life, is everywhere,
and it is my privilege to be a part of this. I can
flow with it. I can accept the peace, perfection, love,
the constant flow of God's eternal blessings into my
life every moment of the day. I can love the Lord
my God with all my heart, with all my mind, with
all my strength, and love my neighbor as myself.

Or I can go back to blocking this flow with negation. *The choice is mine — and the choice is yours.*

Jesus' concept of God is a wonderful inspiration.
Love and forgiveness is the basis of all His teachings. When the world accepts His simple truths,
there will then be peace on earth and good will
among men.

God loves you, and approves of you. Give a
prayer of thanksgiving for all your blessings, and
for the happiness, health, joy, success, and abundance of good which is yours to claim and to express in your life from this day forward.

THE THIRD COMMANDMENT

Jesus gave us still a third and last commandment. This is the most important lesson of all. It encompasses all the others. It is, in fact, the ultimate goal of all mankind. I know of no man of this century who has even appraoched this goal. Dr. Schweitzer and Mahatma Ghandi possibly come as close to it as any I can think of at the moment. This third commandment is to "love one another as I have loved you." Jesus' love was completely unselfish. He gave of His love and service to mankind without any thought of personal gain or worldly reward. He made the supreme sacrifice in His love for us, and yet He tells us that we must love one another as He loved us! Think of it! It is a challenge to the world today, and if the world is to survive, we must accept this challenge. We must love our neighbors across the street and across the sea, and we must do it without a thought of what they can do for us financially, politically or any other way. Our love must be unselfish and complete.

You may say this is impossible. Jesus did it, and

then said that these things that He did, we shall do also, and even greater works than these. To do anything we must make a start, and the time to start is now — today. We can do this by forgetting ourselves and our own wants for a time, and doing a good turn for our neighbor next door. We can pray for others as well as for ourselves. We can pray for the light of love and truth to reach the hearts of the leaders of all nations. God is love, and love is the most powerful force on this earth. It is more powerful than *anything* man can create. The power of prayer is unlimited. Pray for world peace and have faith that your prayer will be answered.

When we reach such a plane of spiritual consciousness that we pray for others without thought of reward, and give of ourselves and our worldly goods to help our neighbor, we suddenly realize we have *found* the secret of true happiness. We find our own troubles and worries and frustrations vanishing when we put into practice in our everyday lives this commandment to love one another. Jesus gave the world the Gold Key to happiness. As each of us comes closer to the ultimate goal of this third commandment, we do our part in making this a better world.

BRIDGE TO A BETTER LIFE

So let go and let God take charge of your life *today*. Substitute faith for fear, love for distrust and hate, and put right thoughts in place of worry thoughts. Be tolerant, kindly, and helpful to others as we all journey through this life experience together. Seek ye first the Kingdom of Heaven and all the good things of this world will flow to you in a never ending stream. Today is the day and now is the time to claim your Divine heritage.

WHAT IS THE PURPOSE OF LIFE?

I believe everyone should have a goal in life; something to strive for, something to work for. We should make up our minds what it is we want, set our course, and keep headed in one direction.

Too many people today are frittering their precious days away as though they were in a boat with no rudder. Mostly they drift with the tide, and when they start the motor they go around in circles, head out to nowhere, or crack up on the rocks.

God didn't put us here on earth just to vegetate. Some folks get up in the morning, go to work, come home tired, eat the evening meal, watch a few TV westerns, put out the cat, go to bed, get up in the morning, go to work, etc., over and over. Same pattern, same thoughts, same old bills to pay every month and, as some put it, "the same old rat race." At the end of our life span (and it is a relatively short one), just what have we really accomplished? What have we done that is worth while?

Have you ever given serious thought as to why you are here? Where you came from? Where you are going when you finish your three score years and ten? What is the purpose of life? If we go through life without a purpose and without a goal, how can we hope to be truly happy?

We have a right to think about life and about death. We should search out the true purpose of living. We should have a definite reason as to why it is best to love God and our neighbors; why we should live as nearly a Christlike life as we possibly can. Not just because we think it's the moral thing to do, or because the preacher said we had better be good or evil will befall us. It goes far deeper than this.

Life, as I see it, is like a school. Some of us are in the first grade, some in the second or third grade, or even in high school. Those in the higher grades have had to earn them. We have lessons to learn and we are put here to master them. Jesus outlined the sort of life we must lead to graduate eventually into the Christ man. He demonstrated that this could be done, and said that the works He has done, we shall do also.

If we think we are very far along the way, just look around us. Men are still fighting and killing one another, cheating and stealing to attain more wealth or worldly power, ruthless and cruel to their fellow men. These people are still in the kindergarten of the school of real attainment. Those of us who just drift along are possibly in the first grade, and until we start to devote ourselves seriously to mastering the lessons of life, we'll stay right there.

Life has a purpose and only one purpose; it is our soul-growth. We must *grow* spiritually. This is the only thing that really counts in this world, and we had better be about it. It is something we must do for ourselves. No one else can do it for us.

I realize that there are some who believe that when we die, we do one of two things; either we go to the place where it is very, very hot and we sizzle for eternity, or we go where the streets are paved with gold, sit on a little pink cloud, wear a solid gold crown and spend our days playing on a harp, taking a 'coffee break' now and then to drink milk and eat honey!

I'm afraid I can't go along with this idea. We are told that life is eternal, and I believe that it is. I think that if we have learned some of the lessons of this life, — love, forgiveness, true accomplishment of anything that has been a real help to mankind, — we can expect a promotion to the next grade when we pass on. If we haven't even tried to attain a higher understanding of life, we stay in the same grade. If we have led a life of hate, of suspicion, of greed, of wrongdoing, we will be demoted to a lower grade and have to overcome these evils in the next life.

I am not making a case either for or against reincarnation. There are millions of wonderful people on this earth who accept this, and I have no quarrel with them. Whether we come back here again and again and again, to learn our lessons, or whether we have to learn them in another world or planet doesn't concern me. The thing that does concern me is this — It is up to me to go just as far as I can during this lifetime to attain a higher spiritual consciousness; to apply the teachings of Jesus in my everyday living; to apply them to my business, to my home life, to my social life, to every part of every day.

When the time comes for me to shuffle off this mortal coil, I expect to take up right where I left off and go on from there. I don't know how many years or eons I have lived in the past, or how long it will take for me to reach the goal of perfection that is the ultimate goal for all mankind, but I do know the direction in which I am headed.

It is a wonderful challenge to see how much we can improve our lives, and we can start *today*. We must be about this business of doing away with the Adam man and putting Christ first and foremost in our everyday living. Life is not measured by the money you leave for your heirs to fight over; it is measured by what you have *given* to life rather than what you have *taken*. It is measured by how you have best used the talents God has given you. It is measured by the love and joy you have given others. We all have to face the problems of life as a child faces problems in his lessons at school. As we stated earlier in this text, it isn't the problem or challenge we face that is so important; it is how we face it, rise above it, and overcome it.

As we advance in spiritual understanding, we come to know it isn't always the so-called big things that are most important. The friendly smile or cheery word you give to a friend may be the most important event of your day. So let us set our course toward a better, finer, cleaner life, and know with absolute assurance that this is the only way to make true progress toward our ultimate goal. Whether we make it in a year or a thousand years, we do know this: life is eternal and we are living a happier, more useful and more abundant life in every way if we steer a straight course toward what we know to be right for us, and right for our fellowman.